What's this SHOE

All About?

Changing People's Lives
and
MUCH MORE!

By:

Alvaro Z. Gallegos

Order this book online at www.trafford.com
or email orders@trafford.com

Most Trafford titles are also available at major online book retailers.

Printed in the United States of America.

ISBN: 978-1-4269-7934-7

Library of Congress Control Number: 2011912437

Trafford rev. 09/12/2011

Trafford
PUBLISHING® www.trafford.com

North America & international
toll-free: 1 888 232 4444 (USA & Canada)
phone: 250 383 6864 ♦ fax: 812 355 4082

Dedicated to all the people who

have suffered from the kind of pain

described in the book and don't know the reason for the pain.

This book gives the reason for

the dilemma we are in and answers some of the questions.

FORWARD

America is deeply afflicted by a pandemic of pain. The scourge of debilitating discomfit of the foot, ankle, knee, leg, hip and back is multi-factorial. On a daily basis, a whopping 70 percent of the population of the United States suffers from at least one of these areas of pain, and, not uncommonly more than one.

The "aging process" is often the scapegoat for these discomfits. Others shift the blame to their participation in athletics. All Gallegos believes that "pain' is not an inevitable consequence of living and should be solved rather than rationalized. We can all accept transient discomfits, but should not be burdened by chronic and disabling suffering.

Al has been a competitive runner for thirty years, and has worked in the shoe industry for forty-three years. When foot and leg pain threatened to sideline him, he began to seek solutions. He spent many years trying to understand what caused the problems that he and so many others were experiencing daily. He consulted with podiatrists, orthopedists, physical medicine specialists, and orthotists and read treatises on related subjects. He experimented with many different solution options, and proudly, always tried to think 'outside the box." The "box" is an antiquated structure which still confines its inhabitants to unsuccessful treatments. The 'box' has captured a stereotypical shoe design and treatment regimen which too often prevents patients from thinking of newer and realistic advances in shoe design. Not uncommonly, today, neither the treatments nor the shoes are really doing the job.

The outcome of Al's work is footwear unlike anything else available today. His new shoe designs are changing people's lives and are fast becoming a demanding "must" for life as a thinking biped.

Read about this man and his amazing quest to understand and abolish the mundane life diminishing pain that people tolerate daily.

Dr. Barry Maron

COVER STORY

At first glance, the Z-CoiL shoe often strikes some people as some kind of gimmick, but this unique line of pain relief footwear is steadily gaining favor with both foot care specialists and regular customers, who have benefited from the technology involved in making this footwear.

The shoe on the cover is called the Freedom 2000, and it is the flagship model from the Z-CoiL Shoe Company of Albuquerque, New Mexico.

The shoe is definitely not a gimmick, and when you put the shoe on, you know **immediately** that it isn't a gimmick!

The shoe was designed to reduce all the impact to the body as we walk or run, and it does a great job of doing just that. The spring is so strong, you will notice that the spring will return the energy you have put in the shoe as you walk.

The full line of Z-CoiL products is designed with a rigid built in orthotic, which gives the shoe unmatched support across the middle part of the foot. In addition to the great support and unmatched cushioning of the spring, the shoes have a cushioned rocker bottom in the forefoot. This allows for the wearer to roll right off the front of the shoe. We encourage anyone that hasn't tried on a Z-CoiL shoe to at least slip on a pair and walk around the block. Any of our dealers will let you do that! You will be pleasantly surprised.

SOME THOUGHTS

I was just thinking about how big an industry this pain relief business is and has continued to grow in volume. Not only has the pain medication business grown, but also the surgical business has increased in volume over the last few years. Great strides have been made on the surgical side. It's great that hips and knees can be replaced so easily, but there can be side effects to the medication and surgical side of solving the pain problem.

It seems almost too simple that a shoe can solve so many of the problems mentioned above.

The Athletic Shoe

Perhaps we could say that the difference between "fashion shoes" and athletic shoes is that the shoes that are "good for you" offer more cushioning, though we will see that many claims for good cushioning are not well founded. Some "good for you" shoes are really expensive, but we'll see that price is no guarantee of quality.

The key to developing a shoe that meets the needs of the human body is to provide adequate cushioning and adequate support. Let's look at just a couple of the shoes on the market that claim to be good for you.

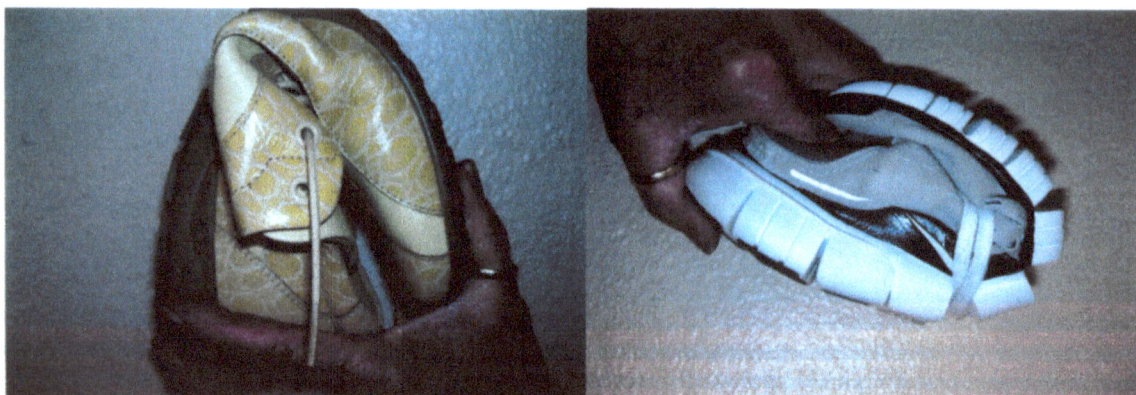

When it comes to the injuries that hurt our lower extremities, almost no one is asking the why question. This lack of curiosity is the more surprising, because there are even activity-specific injuries: basketball players have high rates of knee and ankle problems, for example, and runners demanding help? The major reason is that athletes expect to suffer injuries. They believe injuries are an inevitable part of sports activity. But, it just doesn't have to be so!

In another section of this book, I discuss a way to alleviate the pain of arthritis in any of our joints by lubricating with a natural oil.

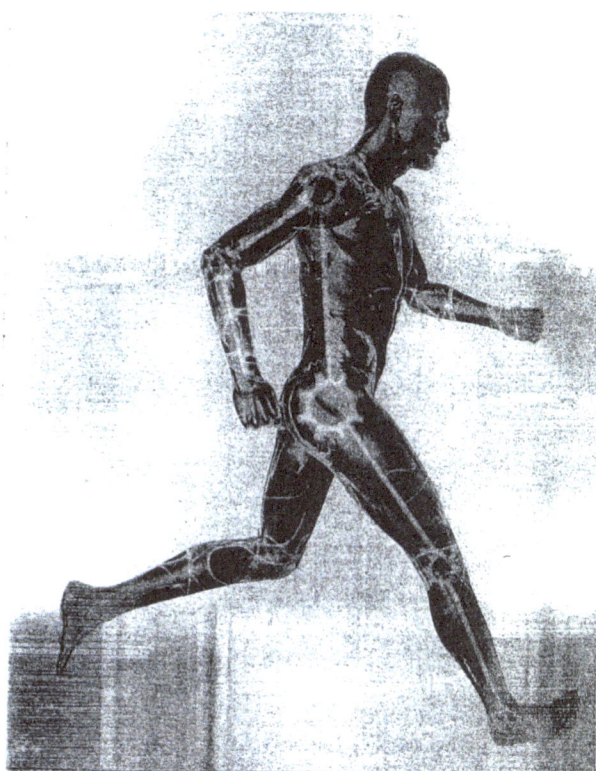

Model of the Human Body

The body is pretty compact, and we start out life with great joints and very little cushioning, but with the onset of cement floors and walks, the effect of many miles on concrete has to have an effect on our bodies.

Innovative Footwear Provides Relief from Pain

By Carla Salizzoni

At first glance, **Z-CoiL®** shoes often strike people as some kind of gimmick. But this unique line of Pain Relief Footwear™ is steadily gaining ground among foot care professionals who are recognizing the functional benefits of its design. Invented in Albuquerque by a runner in his 50s who was continually plagued by running injuries, the footwear is engineered to reduce the damaging effects of repetitive impact on the body by acting basically as shock absorbers for the feet. For years, Z-CoiL customers have reported significant relief from many painful ailments of the feet, knees, hips, and lower back that are typically caused by overuse, injury, or disease.

Built for Pain Relief

The most notable feature of Z-CoiL shoes, of course, is the conical steel coil under the heel. Like a shock absorber in a car, this "spring suspension system," together with dense cushioning under the metatarsal heads, greatly reduces the shock of impact when walking or running.

In fact, a study performed by Los Alamos National Laboratories found that Z-CoiL shoes reduced the rate of impact to the body by up to 50 percent, while also delivering a 40 to 50 percent kinetic energy return. The report concludes, "The initial impact forces appear to be less abrupt in the Z-CoiL shoes, resulting in a reduction of the jarring effect to the foot and lower leg as the heel impacts the ground."

Similar tests performed by Sandia National Laboratories showed "an increase in cushioning, at various forces, of over 100 percent in the toe box and 50 percent in the heel of a Z-CoiL shoe when compared to [a] name-brand cushioned shoe."

Also built into the shoe is a rigid, three-quarter-length orthotic that performs the same function as the solid frame of a car, providing a stable platform for the shock-absorbing coil. Moreover, this prefabricated orthotic distributes weight evenly across the midfoot and offers excellent support from the heel to the metatarsal heads to address such painful conditions as plantar fasciitis and heel spurs.

A built-in flex-line located directly under the MP joints and a rocker-bottom forefoot work in tandem with the flexible coil to create a smooth, rolling gait. This helps to treat mid-foot and forefoot symptoms and pathology, similar to a custom-made shoe or cast boot rocker sole.

> *A variety of adjustments can be made to Z-Coil footwear to address many different foot and gait issues.*

Addresses a Variety of Conditions

Patients suffering from a wide range of conditions have reported either partial or complete relief from pain after wearing Z-CoiL footwear. According to Kevin Brattain, DPM, of the Illinois Valley Podiatry Group, indications for the footwear can include pain due to arthritis of any lower extremity joint and/or back; general heel pain and plantar fasciitis; pes planus; pes cavus; tendonitis of leg, ankle, or foot; PT tendon dysfunction; limb-length discrepancy; first metatarsal phalangeal joint pain; and mid-foot, rear foot and ankle arthrodesis. In addition, he finds that patients who suffer from non-specific complaints of repetitive stress, pain

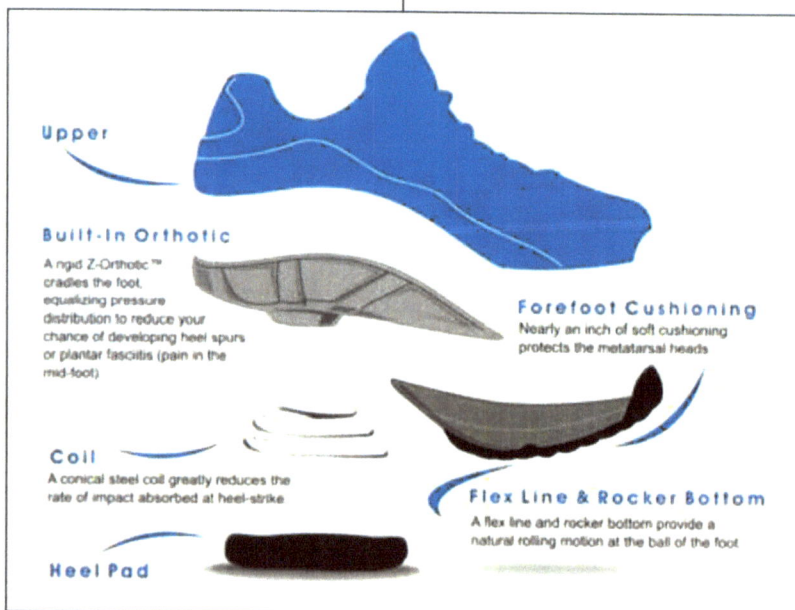

Upper

Built-In Orthotic
A rigid Z-Orthotic™ cradles the foot, equalizing pressure distribution to reduce your chance of developing heel spurs or plantar fasciitis (pain in the mid-foot)

Coil
A conical steel coil greatly reduces the rate of impact absorbed at heel-strike

Heel Pad

Forefoot Cushioning
Nearly an inch of soft cushioning protects the metatarsal heads

Flex Line & Rocker Bottom
A flex line and rocker bottom provide a natural rolling motion at the ball of the foot

Z-CoiL® footwear components

Innovative Footwear...

when standing, and "painful or weak legs" also benefit.

Dr. J Lee, a Chiropractor in Arlington, Texas, writes, "Tremendous shock absorption ability reduces incidents of low back, sciatic, knee and foot pain in several of my patients. I feel very good about referring my chiropractic patients for the possible therapeutic value of the shoes. The shoes keep some of my more difficult cases moving. I wear nothing but Z-CoiL shoes on my feet all day, every day in the office!"

Nurses, known to spend long hours on their feet on hard floors, have proven to be the most common, and often the most devoted, Z-CoiL customers. Christina Farley, a registered nurse in Metropolis, Illinois, says, "I have had a problem with heel spurs and plantar fasciitis for over four years. I have a huge collection of athletic shoes, but nothing can take the place of my Z-CoiL shoes. They truly have saved my feet and career."

Although a Z-CoiL footwear distributor himself, with stores in both Peoria, Illinois, and Davenport, Iowa, Dr. Brattain stresses that Z-CoiL footwear is not for everyone and should be used judiciously. "As with any treatment modality, Z-CoiL footwear is not a universal cure. I consider the shoes to be one more option that may help an existing treatment plan result in an even better outcome," he says.

Z-CoiL® Freedom 2000

Adjustable for a Custom Fit

A variety of adjustments can be made to Z-CoiL footwear to address many different foot and gait issues. For example, the orthotic can be widened to allow for extremely wide or flat feet, and the upper can be shaped to fit those with very narrow heels, bunions, or hammertoes. Foam inserts can be added to accommodate high arches, corns, or large calluses. The heel coils come in varying degrees of stiffness, to suit patients of different body weights. And patients are able to insert their own custom orthotics into the shoes as well.

Further adjustments can be made

> *The Z-CoiL product line features many different styles, including athletic shoes, clogs, dress shoes, sandals and work boots.*

to the heel coil to address leg-length discrepancies, and to help compensate for cases of over-pronation and over-supination.

The design of the coil also presents stronger and weaker sides, depending on the way the coil is rotated. For example, severe over-pronation can be countered by turning the strongest side of the coil toward the inside of the foot to help normalize the person's gait.

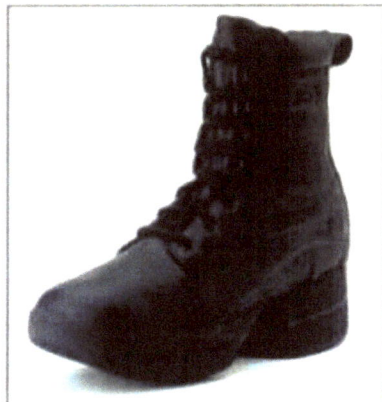

Z-Duty Work Boot

Because the Z-CoiL Footwear company's goal is to achieve the greatest pain-relief benefits possible with its footwear, Z-CoiL Pain Relief Footwear is sold only through authorized distributors who are specially trained to custom-fit the shoes. In fact, Z-CoiL counts podiatrists, certified pedorthists, chiropractors, and physical therapists among its distributors. There are currently over 140 authorized Z-CoiL stores in the U.S. across 40 states, as well as Canada and Puerto Rico.

The Z-CoiL product line features many different styles, including athletic shoes, clogs, dress shoes, sandals and work boots. Certain styles come with an Enclosed Heel System™ to address workplace safety concerns, where objects are more likely to get caught in an open coil. The molded foam material that encases the coil slows the speed at which the coil compresses, which dampens its shock-absorbing capabilities to some degree, although a stiffer coil also proves useful when a person is picking up heavy objects. These work shoes also come with or without an ANSI-rated steel toe.

For more information about the shoes, to locate authorized Z-CoiL stores, or to learn about available franchise opportunities, visit the company's website at www.zcoil.com, call 800-268-6239, or *circle #181 on the reader service card.*

Chapter 1

Problems: This Is the Situation

Lifelong health is a major concern for many people today. Our focus on the prevention of disease is growing. We're no longer satisfied with simply treating problems after things have gone wrong. Instead, we're looking for ways to achieve and maintain wellness, ways to stay healthy and fully functioning, and the number of people thinking about wellness is growing by leaps and bounds. Wellness is big business!

Is there anyone out there who doesn't know the importance of regular exercise in maintaining a strong, healthy body? Probably not. But, there's one element involved in getting that exercise that has been pretty much ignored. We've paid almost no attention to the crucial role played by having good strong feet and legs and a good strong back in staying healthy and active.

In fact, do we even know *how* to make sure we have those good strong feet and legs and back? Absolutely not! The sad truth is that we treat our feet like dirt! And, instead of improving, our feet are in worse shape now than people's feet were thirty or forty years ago. A few numbers will give you a picture of how bad things are. Fifty-nine million Americans have foot problems, according to the national Center for Health Statistics, while an independent survey done for the American Podiatric Medical Association (APMA) found that 76 percent of Americans have had foot problems in the last year. Worse, 42 percent of men and 39 percent of women think having pain is "normal."

How can this be?

Let's look at the big picture. Has anything changed in the last generation or so that would affect foot, leg, and back pain? Yes! Some very important things have changed. For one thing, people are bigger than they used to be. And, a whopping 62 percent of all Americans are overweight! Greater weight and longer bones put more stress on the lower extremities. And, people are living longer, too, so their bones and ligaments need to last longer if they hope to have a high quality lifestyle in their later years. For another, people are walking and standing on hard surfaces more – they may stand for twelve-hour shifts on concrete floors, for example. And, finally, the amount of exercise that most people get is less. Daily living requires little physical exertion now, and despite the public health announcements and our general knowledge about it, most people do not participate in regular exercise programs. Some are even complacent about it!

Did you know.....

Obesity and diabetes are still on the rise in the US. The Albuquerque Journal on New Year's Day, 2003, reported that more than 44 million Americans were obsess and 16.7 million people had diagnosed diabetes in 1001, according to a study done by the Centers for Disease Control and Prevention. That's an obesity rate of 20.9 percent, up from 19.8 percent the year before, while the rate of diagnosed diabetes rose to 7.0 percent from 7.3 percent.

These lifestyle changes have their effects on a very complex machine; the foot has twenty-six bones, thirty-three joints, thirty-eight muscles, and a network of more than a hundred tendons, muscles, and ligaments. Our two feet together contain about a quarter of all the bones in the body!

When we walk, we land on each foot with almost double our weight. When we run, we land with almost triple our weight each time we hit the ground. That's a lot of impact for us to absorb with our backs, our legs, our knees and our feet. It's no wonder we hurt!

The increasing numbers of foot, leg, and back care specialists is further evidence of the epidemic of pain. Today there are about seventy-five thousand members of the American Physical Therapists Association, almost sixteen thousand members in the American Podiatrists Association, some fifty-eight thousand chiropractors, and over thirteen hundred certified pedorthists, not to mention all the acupuncturists, massage therapists, and other health specialists who are needed to keep us up and walking. The number of specialists and professionals who take care of all the problems we have is growing every day, because painful and debilitating conditions that affect the lower extremities are rampant. It's a growth industry! And, this industry will continue to grow, unless we understand and solve the problem.

Everyone, by now, is aware of the fact that when we run, we are impacting the ground with our feet up to five times our weight. Even when we are just walking or strolling casually, we can impact the ground as much as twice the amount we weigh. So, you can see that even a 120 pound woman will impact the ground with 240 pounds of pressure on the one foot. Also, if that step is taken on concrete or tile floors, the impact is felt all through the calcium chain of bones. If there is any weakness in the chain of bones and in tendons, we start to break down there.

The current crop of footwear companies have continually designed for fashion and not for function. I do think the designs of the new current styles are really great. Also, the materials that are used are really light in weight and make the running shoe feel good....when you first try it out, but then the problems start. Since almost every shoe is built with no mid-foot support, the little cushioning that they have will not work. The materials that are used for cushioning are really dangerous since they have no energy return and no possibility of cushioning without the rigid foot form (orthotic) above the "supposed" cushioning.

The cushioning technology in the modern automobile would not work if the automobile did not have a strong and rigid frame (like the orthotic in a shoe). This frame provides a base for all the cushioning.

Most physicians and foot doctors acknowledge that repeated impact to the body can be detrimental. In fact, one of the first things a doctor will recommend to anyone with arthritis or diabetes is to lose weight to reduce the impact to our body as we walk. Herniated discs or torn muscles or tendons also require much caution on the individual to reduce impact.

There are a few ways that we can reduce impact, and I guess we could review those, even though some are impractical, such as using a trampoline, having balloons tied to our waist, or using wheels such as roller blades or skates.

Really, the most practical method of cushioning our body would be to make our shoes with great support and a lot of cushioning.

These are some of the alternative methods of cushioning our body as we move around. Of course, these are not very practical, but this is the kind of cushioning we need –

Using a Parachute!   **Using a Mattress!**   **Using a Trampoline!**

But, we can't confine our activities to these special locations for everything we do in our lives; we need a solution that stays with us wherever we go. It seems that the best – the only – place to start is to develop an apparatus for our feet that would cut the impact *at the exact point* that we touch the surface of the earth. The only place we can reliably provide the body with cushioning and support is in our shoes. Nothing else is going to work.

This is what we feel like in most shoes that are now currently made --
It's like jumping on concrete!

It's very widely believed that great strides have been made in shoe design for athletes in recent years. In fact, it is assumed that once you get the right kind of shoe for the activity you undertake – a shoe for running or for soccer or for cross-training – there is little else to concern you, other than getting the right size in that shoe. This is a dangerous assumption. The midfoot area of athletic shoes is weaker than that of most other shoes on the market, but *because we assume they'll help us more than our "regular" shoes*, we wear our athletic shoes more than those other shoes, and so we get injured more.

It used to be that we only wore athletic shoes for athletics. Now, many people wear them to the exclusion of everything else. Choosing the right shoe for the special activity that we have in mind is really pretty difficult, because most athletic shoes have no real support nor do they have real good cushioning.

The picture above shows two very active basketball players that are extremely active for at least one hour, and the shoes they wear have no ankle or foot support and no cushioning. When the problems arise, then we resort to pain pills and/or surgery. Great options!

The approach taken to preventing accidents to the lower extremities today is non-existent, but we do have many, many treatments for injuries to the foot, ankle, knee, and back, but no one has been focusing on designing an apparatus with the support and cushioning that will really protect these sensitive parts of our bodies during the activities we choose to undertake, including those activities that are, in fact, essential to maintaining good health throughout our lives.

So, what would we have to do to come up with an apparatus, a device to make it safe to walk or run or just stand without being hurt by the impact that can affect everything from our feet to our backs? Well, we know now that almost all the injuries that affect the lower extremities are caused by – first, a lack of cushioning and, second, lack of support.

Earlier attempts to cushion the body

A GOOD SHOE

You have heard people say, "I only buy good shoes," or have seen retailers advertize that they sell shoes that are good for you. Let's talk about what makes a good shoe.

Any shoe that is made should be able to protect our feet and reduce the impact to the body as we walk or run. Since the foot itself has no flex from the metatarsal bones (right behind the toes) to the heel, the footwear should have no flex anywhere in that medial area. So many problems can be the result of a less than rigid mid-foot shoe. In addition to the rigid mid-foot, the shoe should have cushioning to absorb all the impact as we walk or run.

Of all the shoes I used for running, none of the shoes had enough cushioning, and I was getting hurt all the time. I have to mention here that all the cushioning in the world, without a firm base, results in very little cushioning.

The lack of knowledge required to provide stability (support), cushioning, and energy return in footwear is truly amazing. In the April 2005 issue of "Bio Mechanics," there is a big article about reinventing the soccer shoe. The article is about the need for a soccer shoe that is stable, yet flexible, lightweight, and has a high coefficient of friction when the wearer strikes the ball to get spin on the soccer on the soccer shoe. All soccer shoes are designed to be very lightweight. They also provide no cushioning or mid-foot support at all in order to remain lightweight. They do acknowledge that it is very difficult to develop a shoe with good cushioning and stability. In fact, they state that good cushioning and stability are incompatible in footwear. Certainly, if you begin with the premise that cushioning and support are incompatible in footwear, you would not design a shoe with great cushioning and good support at the same time.

Not only are soccer shoes designed with very little mid-foot support, most athletic shoes, many dress shoes, and even work boots are designed with very little mid-foot support. In fact, Nike has become so frustrated; they are now making the "Nike Free," a shoe that has no support and no cushioning. It doesn't even pretend to have any of those qualities.

THE JOINTS OF OUR BODY

If anyone tells you that you are bone on bone in your hips, ankles, or knees, they are right. Take a look at the pictures of the knee, hip, or foot and you will see that there is very little space from one bone to the next. What the joints have is a thin layer of cartilage separating most of the joints, and the joint is lubricated with synovial fluid, which allows us to move all the joints easily. Cartilage and synovial fluid do not have much cushioning qualities, so when we walk or run on hard surfaces, especially concrete floors or walks, we are stressing the joints. Even though we have cushioned rugs and carpets, we walk more often in areas that don't have any cushioning, such as sidewalks, shopping centers, outdoor basketball courts, tennis courts, etc. It is no wonder that we develop pain over a period of time.

You will not read or hear in any publication that maybe impact could be the reason for our pain. You will read that we have been making great strides in improving footwear. I do know that a lot of lip service has been given to addressing the pain problem, but the technology remains the same.

Structure of the Hip

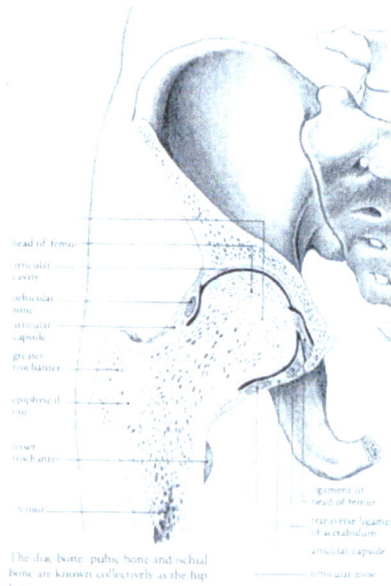

Verticle Section of Knee

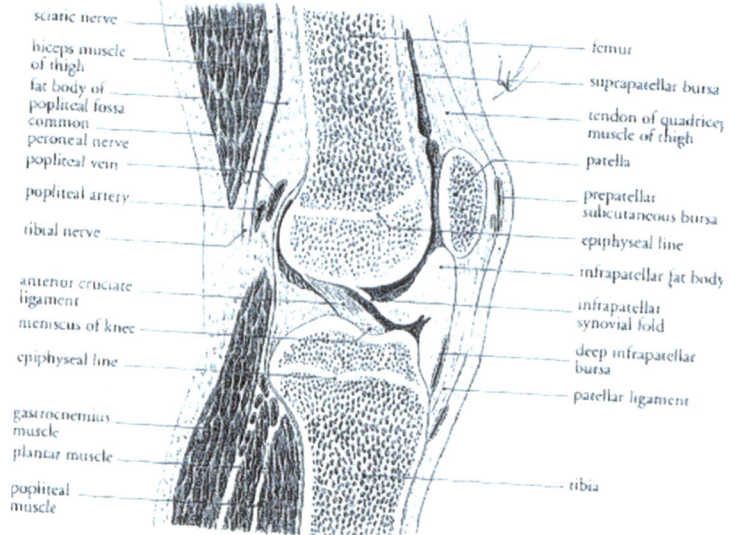

sciatic nerve
biceps muscle of thigh
fat body of popliteal fossa
common peroneal nerve
popliteal vein
popliteal artery
tibial nerve
anterior cruciate ligament
meniscus of knee
epiphyseal line
gastrocnemius muscle
plantar muscle
popliteal muscle

femur
suprapatellar bursa
tendon of quadriceps muscle of thigh
patella
prepatellar subcutaneous bursa
epiphyseal line
infrapatellar fat body
infrapatellar synovial fold
deep infrapatellar bursa
patellar ligament
tibia

head of femur
articular cavity
ischiadic bone
articular capsule
greater trochanter
epiphyseal line
lesser trochanter
femur
ligament of head of femur
transverse ligament of acetabulum
articular capsule
articular bone

The iliac bone, pubis bone and ischial bone are known collectively as the hip

Section of Achilles

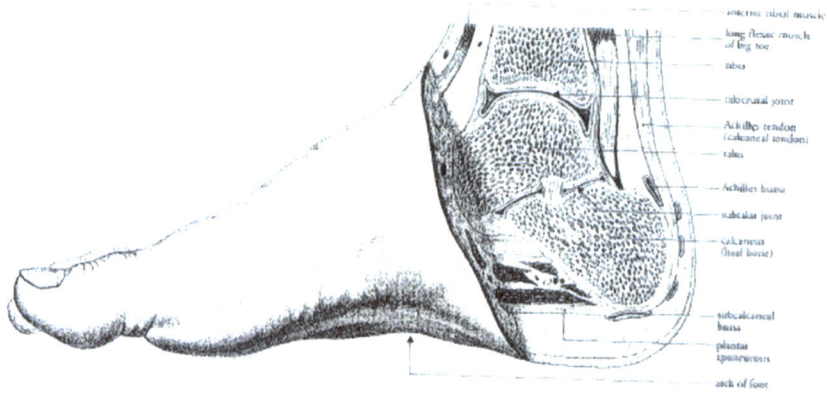

internal tibial muscle
long flexor muscle of big toe
tibia
talocrural joint
Achilles tendon (calcaneal tendon)
talus
Achilles bursa
subtalar joint
calcaneus (heel bone)
subcalcaneal bursa
plantar aponeurosis
arch of foot

TALKING ABOUT PAIN

Pain is something we all have in common and experience, whether rich or poor, whether young or old. More than one quarter of the nation's adults suffer from persistent pain, the National Center for Health Statistics says.

The ultimate number of people with back pain in a period of one year is approximately 59 million, and that's only back pain! The other kinds of natural pains we have in a larger percentage are knee pain and foot pain.

When the National Center for Health mentions how many people suffer from chronic pain, they can give us a pretty accurate figure of how many suffer on a yearly basis, but what they usually don't give is the reason for the high numbers of people in pain. I've waited on and fitted many people, who come into our Albuquerque store, into Z-CoiL shoes. I've witnessed these people, who are in pain, walk a few steps and have their pain leave them. This tells me a couple of things:

1. Reducing the impact to the body is a very essential key to relieving the pain to the body.

2. We really don't think about how much pressure we put on our feet, knees, and back as we walk.

This whole scenario is accelerated when we walk on cement or on any hard surface. And, as I show in this book, when we walk or run, we are bone-on-bone, except for a little cartilage and synovial fluid to allow the joints to more easily.

You can tell, as a nation, we take a very aggressive approach to solving the pain problem, because the amount of money spent on prescription medication (pain killers) is in the billions of dollars! Heck, you can tell it's a big business. There is a drugstore on every corner in most towns. According to the market research firm, Information Resources, Inc., Americans spent more than $2.4 billion on non-prescription painkillers between November 2007 and November 2008. The federal agency for Healthcare Research and Quality reports that 57 million people bought prescription painkillers in 2006, spending a total of $13.2 billion. You hear this so often – Ask your doctor if this medication is right for you. That is presupposing that anything, and maybe everything, that causes pain to us is due to a chemical or medical imbalance in our bodies.

The addition of arthritic pain to the equation only adds to the total amount of pain killers we buy on a yearly basis.

All drugs have dangerous side effects, which are printed in small print.

All of these so-called medications for pain do not solve the problem or the reason for the pain. One of the major reasons for back pain is the amount of impact the body gets as we walk or run. The body has so many more physical challenges that easily 40%-50% of all problems are due to impact. Right now, there are only a handful of shoe companies that have footwear that truly reduces the impact to the body and that supports the feet properly at the same time.

The Z-CoiL shoe is the only footwear that is built with a good rigid orthotic that really supports the foot, and at the same time provides ¾ inch of great cushioning with the spring.

All the joints in the body will enjoy the benefits of the great cushioning, and so many of our customers have been able to rid their bodies of the dangerous medications they are taking.

The pharmaceutical companies have such a strong lobby with the federal government that they are allowed to call their pain killers medication and that by using these so-called medications, it will resolve the reason for the pain. **Pain killers do not solve the reason for the pain**, so we just use more and more painkillers.....Soon, we are addicted.

Once in a while a certain pill is banned or a drug company is told to issue stronger warnings about the dangers of using pain medication. Last year alone, 160,000 people died of prescription medication, and many more are hospitalized for overuse of drugs.

According to the Arthritis Foundation -- **Prescription drugs are the fourth cause of death in the United States!** "Old age is not a time of life, it is a condition of the body. It is not time that ages the body, it is abuse that does." ~ Herbert Shelton.

COMPARATIVE CAUSES OF DEATH. ANNUAL AVERAGE IN THE U. S.

Heart Disease	724,859
Cancer	541,532
Stroke	158,448
Adverse Reactions To Prescription Drugs 2 million additional injuries were caused by adverse reactions to prescription drugs	100,000 to 160,000 ★
Chronic Obstructive Pulmonary Disease	112, 584
Pneumonia/Influenza	91,871
Diabetes	64,751
Automobile Accidents	39,325
Suicide	30,575
Nephritis, nephrotic syndrome, and nephrosis	26,182
Chronic Liver Disease and Cirrhosis	25,192
Food Contamination	9,100
Boating Accidents	2,034
Household Cleaners	74
Acute Pesticide Poisoning	12
All Vitamins	0
Amino acids	0
Commercial Herbal Products	0

Sources of Data: 1998, National Vital Statistics Reports, Vol. 48, No. 11 and Journal of the American Medical Association (April 1998) 1995: American Association of Poison Control Centers, National Center for Health Statistic Centers for Disease Control, March of Dimes, Consumer Product Safety Commission, FDA Reports.

Lisa's Comments:

Pretty shocking isn't it, to think that the FDA is seeking to regulate the innocuous herbal supplement industry, yet is still allowing the sale of toxic prescription drugs. Just look at the most recent drug controversy, when popular painkiller drug Vioxx was pulled from the market in September last year after being found to double cardiovascular risks, with over 27,000 reported deaths resulting from that one drug alone. Celebrex and other Cox-2 inhibitors are soon to follow! How many more drugs out there are doing this kind of damage, yet are still dispensed whimsically by our drug companies. Any prescription drug puts a strain on the liver, the organ responsible for detoxifying our body. Eventually the liver cannot possibly process all the toxins we are constantly pumping into our systems, from the environment (polluted air and water), the toxic foods we eat (processed, packaged foods, red meats, and heavy fats), and the toxic drugs we take, and our cells end up overloaded with toxins. The state of our cellular health dictates our energy levels, resistance against disease, and overall health and well-being. If our cells are sick, we become sick.

Therefore, it is vitally important that we follow the Hippocratic oath: *"Let food be your medicine. Let medicine be your food,"* and only put foods and substances into our bodies that are going to cleanse rather than clog our cells, and therefore ensure optimal health and energy!

"Disease, in my opinion, how prejudicial whatsoever its causes may be to the body, is no more than a vigorous effort of nature to throw off morbidic matter and thus recover the patient." Thomas Snydenham, M.D.

HealthNewsDigest.com article, dated 10/18/2004 – *"**Survey Shows 70 Percent of Rheumatoid Arthritis Patients Receiving Treatment Are Still Impaired Every Day**"* -- Despite tremendous advances in treatments available for rheumatoid arthritis (RA), a nationwide survey commissioned by the Arthritis Foundation shows that 70 percent of adults in the United States with RA still experience joint pain, stiffness and fatigue on a daily basis. Results also reveal that more than one-third rank their quality of life at only a five out of ten at best."

"In an effort to identify unmet needs of the RA community with regard to treatment options and quality of life, the Arthritis Foundation, in collaboration with Harris Interactive, surveyed 500 adults with RA. The most common medications used to treat RA include disease-modifying antirheumatic drugs (DMARDs) and biologic response modifiers (BRMs). Half of the people surveyed report that some symptoms, such as joint pain; stiffness; and swelling are reduced by the medication; however, 49 percent report they continue to modify their daily household activities as a result of their arthritis. Despite significant improvements in treatment for RA over the past ten years, other findings of the survey include: Nearly 70 percent of adults with RA experience pain on a daily basis. More than 50 percent are either extremely concerned or very concerned about their ability to take care of themselves or about the likelihood of becoming disabled. Three or four who are taking DMARDS or BRMs are extremely interested or very interested in talking to their physician about new RA treatments."

In pain? You're not alone.

One in four adults have persistent pain, a new focus of doctors

BY ROCHELLE SHARPE

MORE THAN one-quarter of the nation's adults suffer from persistent pain, the National Center for Health Statistics says. About 74 million deal with pain that lasts more than a day — and the center estimates more than 42% of those people experience pain that lasts longer than a year.

Despite the widespread distress

acute pain condition, it can convert to a chronic pain condition." The nervous system can lock itself into a pattern that is hard to change, he says.

Treating pain is complicated as well as controversial. Relatively few doctors specialize in treating it, Rowe says, and patients often wind up with differing advice from different types of doctors. Meanwhile, doctors have been sued for undertreating pain and

WHERE IT HURTS
The National Center for Health Statistics reports that during a three-month period in 2007:

57 million adults had persistent back pain

29 million adults had neck pain

27.4 million adults had headaches

DID YOU KNOW?

Chronic pain costs **$100 billion a year in lost income**, lost productivity and medical expenses.

caused by pain, scientists and doctors have only recently begun to focus on pain, says Will Rowe, CEO of the American Pain Foundation. "It's been seen as a symptom rather than something worthy of a lot of attention," he says, adding that there wasn't a medical school textbook on pain until 1953.

Yet chronic pain costs the nation $100 billion a year in lost income, lost productivity and medical expenses, the pain foundation says.

Now scientists realize pain can be a disease itself. "If you have pain, don't wait to get it treated," Rowe says. "If you don't properly treat an

for prescribing too many narcotics.
In addition:

● **57 million** people bought prescription painkillers in 2006, spending a total of $13.2 billion, reports the federal Agency for Healthcare Research and Quality.

● Americans spent more than $2.4 **billion** on non-prescription painkillers between November 2007 and November 2008, according to the market research firm Information Resources Inc. **W**

ROCHELLE SHARPE *last wrote about the increase in non-English-speaking households in America.*

Pain can be a disease in and of itself?

★ If we start with that conclusion, we will never look elsewhere for the culprit.

As a runner, I have had lots of pain. I found out, as an old runner, that if I use footwear with good support and cushioning, I don't have any more pain.

(Alvaro Gallegos is now 80 and is able to run pain free because of Z-CoiL shoes!)

ORTHOTICS

Use and Abuse

Custom made orthotics or over-the counter orthotics are designed to be an add-on device to use in conjunction with your shoes to prevent injury or to help with the healing of an ongoing injury.

Since most shoes, especially athletic footwear, have very little mid-foot support and also very little cushioning, the need for add-on orthotics has grown to be a large industry.

If a person has problems with current footwear, most over-the-counter orthotics could be of some help. If the decision is to use a custom orthotic, and the footwear you are using does not have adequate or proper cushioning, you will find the orthotic very uncomfortable. The use of orthotics, whether custom made or over-the-counter, are really a short-term solution to a problem most footwear manufacturers have not understood and have not addressed.

An orthotic should be designed to be an integral part of the footwear. The built-in orthotic, to be most effective, should be very rigid. That way, any type of cushioning under the footwear will translate into cushioning across the base of the foot.

Z-CoiL Footwear products are all designed with built-in orthotics eliminating the need for add-on orthotics.

THE FOOT

BUILT-IN ORTHOTIC
Rigid Support:
A key to preventing foot pain!

Achilles tendon may become sore or even tear from a lack of cushioning

Lack of forefoot cushioning can cause fractured metatarsal bones.

These plantar ligaments can be stretched, bruised, or torn if there is poor mid-foot support.

Heel spurs, caused by the plantar ligaments pulling away from the heel bone, are a result of poor support.

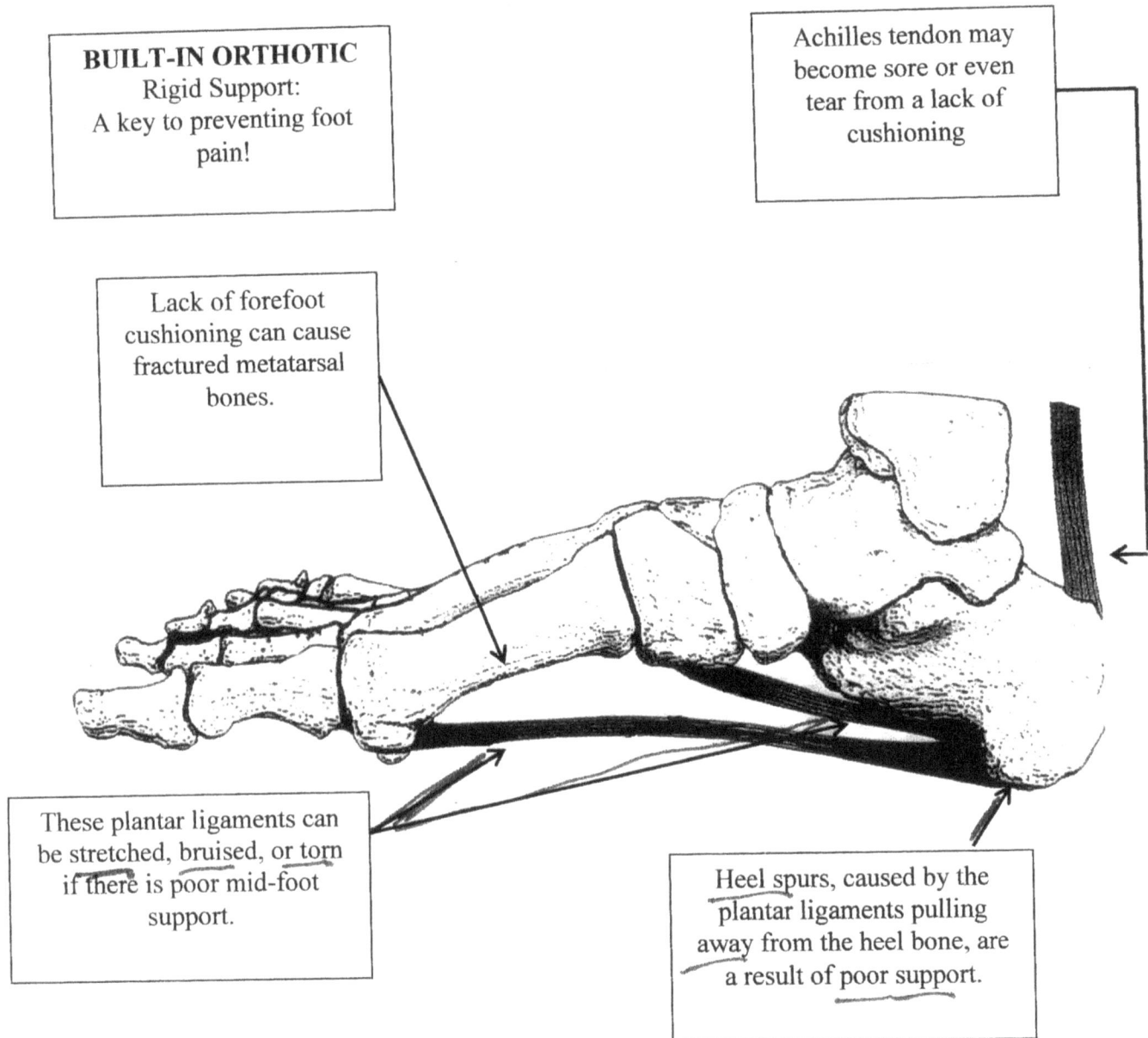

The foot is a very complex piece of equipment that we need to use every

day!

Each foot has twenty-six bones, thirty-three joints, thirty-eight muscles,

and a network of one hundred tendons, muscles and ligaments. If any of these

parts are not well protected, we could start to feel pain that may change the way we walk, causing other problems up the chain of the network – the ankles, knees, and back.

In any given year, almost 65% of Americans have pain of some kind in their feet, according to the American Podiatric Medical Association. It is for this reason I have chosen to talk about the necessity for a shoe that really protects the foot, and at the same time reduces the impact to the body.

If you have a shoe that has no mid-foot support, you are in danger of tearing the plantar ligament. And, with a shoe that has no real support, can the shoe have any real cushioning?

As you will see on the following page, the human spine is beautifully designed and pretty complex – so many nerves, ligaments and muscle surround the spine. There are so many challenges to the spine – Any added weight affects the spine. Lifting and bending will affect the back, but the thing that affects the back the most is the impact on the back as we walk or run. In an article written in Newsweek, April 2004, by Claudia Kalb notes that 80% will have some kind of back pain in their lives, and the number of invasive therapy has spiked to 77% in the last few years. The pain that can be the result of very little cushioning of the body can be herniated discs or slipped vertebrae, causing pinched nerves. Footwear with great cushioning will eliminate so many of the back problems. The footwear should always be the first line of defense for back pain.

atlas
(first cervical vertebra)

axis
(second cervical vertebra)

| 7
Cervical
Vertabra |

cervical
vertebrae

atlas (first
cervical verte

axis (second
cervical verte

| (24)
Intervertebral
Disk |

thoracic
vertebrae

| 14
Thoracic
Vertebra |

| 7
Lumbar
Vertabra |

lumbar
vertebrae

sacrum

| Sacrum |

coccyx

| Coccyx |

Anterior

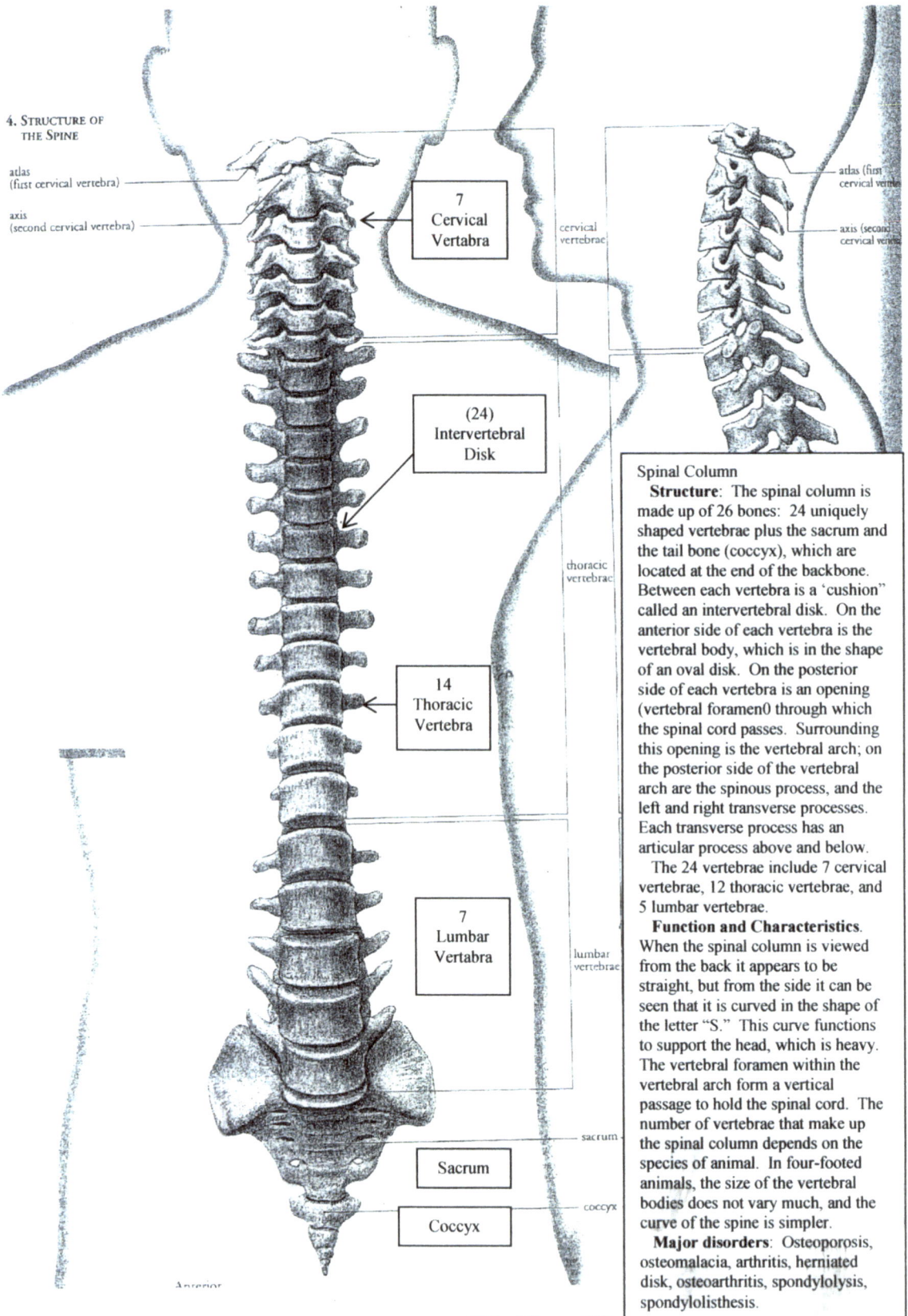

Spinal Column

Structure: The spinal column is made up of 26 bones: 24 uniquely shaped vertebrae plus the sacrum and the tail bone (coccyx), which are located at the end of the backbone. Between each vertebra is a 'cushion" called an intervertebral disk. On the anterior side of each vertebra is the vertebral body, which is in the shape of an oval disk. On the posterior side of each vertebra is an opening (vertebral foramen0 through which the spinal cord passes. Surrounding this opening is the vertebral arch; on the posterior side of the vertebral arch are the spinous process, and the left and right transverse processes. Each transverse process has an articular process above and below.

The 24 vertebrae include 7 cervical vertebrae, 12 thoracic vertebrae, and 5 lumbar vertebrae.

Function and Characteristics. When the spinal column is viewed from the back it appears to be straight, but from the side it can be seen that it is curved in the shape of the letter "S." This curve functions to support the head, which is heavy. The vertebral foramen within the vertebral arch form a vertical passage to hold the spinal cord. The number of vertebrae that make up the spinal column depends on the species of animal. In four-footed animals, the size of the vertebral bodies does not vary much, and the curve of the spine is simpler.

Major disorders: Osteoporosis, osteomalacia, arthritis, herniated disk, osteoarthritis, spondylolysis, spondylolisthesis.

FASHION FOOTWEAR

In the U.S. and many places around the world, we are so enamored with high fashion footwear – so much so that we don't worry whether they are practical or dangerous, so long as they are fashionable. For fun, here are some very ridiculous models of shoes that really are bad for the feet. None of the shoes shown have any cushioning!

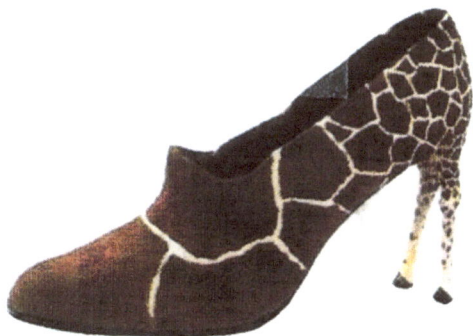

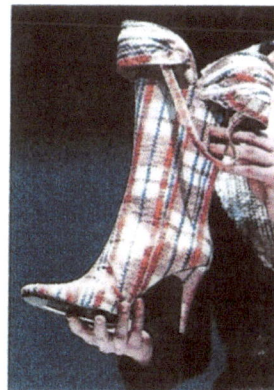

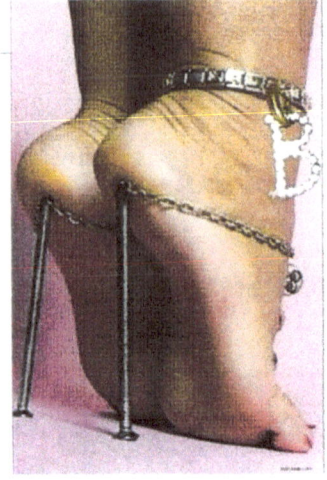

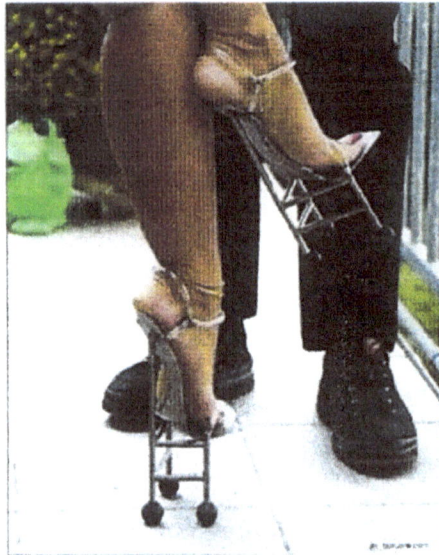

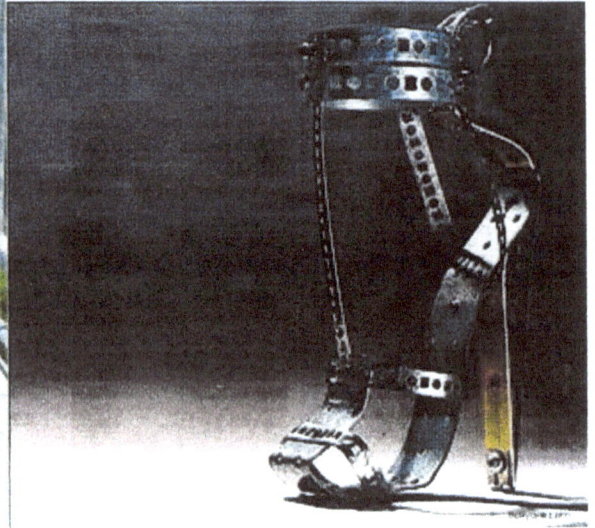

STYLE TRUMPS COMFORT

AND

OTHER OBSERVATIONS

What!

Just as I was completting this book – out came some shoe company promoting light weight non-support footwear. These light flexible minimalist shoes are advertised as a great way to heal their feet. The complete opposite is true. As we walk we put all our weight on our small feet which contains 26 of the smallest bones in our body, and if we don't protect our feet we can have some very serious problems. These minimalist shoes are a podiatrist's dream. I am sure that the foot care business has doubled since these shoes have gone to market.

Another shoe style that recently came out strong, but is now fading fast in popularity, is the rocker bottom shoe. The shoe was being promoted as a shoe that worked many muscles of the legs and buttocks. Yes it was unstable and did cause many problems. A person had to work hard just to stay upright.

Still the best footwear design is one that has a stable foundation "orthotic" and has great cushioning in the heels.

Look at the runners on the following page. They run hitting their heels first which is a comfortable way to walk or run. The shoe needs good cushioning in the heel.
Also,

I must warn you that Z-Coil BioTreck have many imitators. If the spring is a small spring or a stright spring and the shoe can be bent in the arch you probably don't want that kind of a spring shoe. The BioTreck shoe has a built in orthotic and has almost as much cushioning distance as the Z-Coil. That will be a very popular style. You will feel the difference between the Z-Coil and all imitators.

Nothing hurts more
Than running badly

MORE FLOP THAN FLIP

Symbols of summer can be woeful for footsies

By Rachel Saslow
The Washington Post

Sam Hobert, 19, has suffered for his flip-flops.

A few years ago, he broke his right big toe after slamming his foot into a rock while hiking in New Hampshire in his favorite summertime footwear. On a warm day a few weeks ago, the George Washington University freshman was nursing foot blisters, courtesy of a pair of new brown leather 'flops from the Gap.

"It's looks over comfort," he says. "But I'm regretting it a little bit, I'm not gonna lie."

It's springtime and flip-flops — the airy sandal with the distinctive thwack-thwack soundtrack — are back, much to the frustration of podiatrists (but to the delight of their billing departments). Wearing flip-flops can cause problems from stubbed toes and cuts to overuse injuries such as foot stress fractures.

Now that the weather is warm, says Howard Osterman, a podiatrist who has practiced in Washington for 20 years, he will see at least one patient with a flip-flop injury every day through September.

The No. 1 problem he sees from the shoes are overuse injuries such as stress fractures of the metatarsals, the five long bones that reach out to the toes. A stress fracture happens after constant, repetitive stress to a bone and is generally treated with rest, more-supportive shoes and perhaps a walking boot.

Many of the less-expensive flip-flop styles consist of just a flat piece of rubber and the toe thong. The lack of arch support can cause another common foot injury: plantar fasciitis, inflammation of the thick band of tissue along the bottom of the foot that causes a stabbing pain, especially in the heel. People with flatter arches are more prone to such overuse injuries because they need more support for their muscles and ligaments, Osterman says.

Flip-flops also leave the feet unprotected and exposed to the elements, which can mean cold toes,

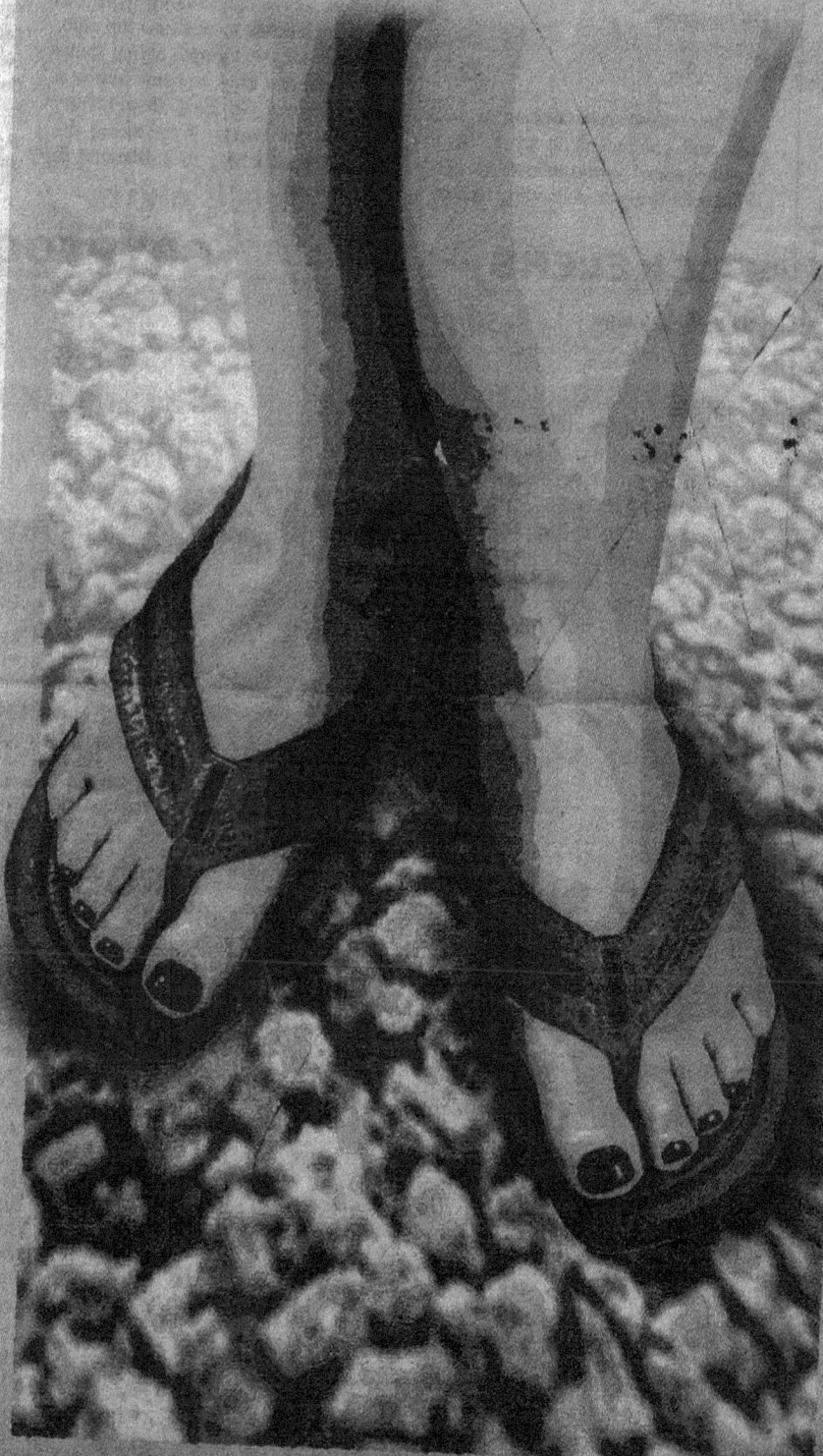

SQUEAKY JOINTS? LUBRICATE THEM!

A BOUT WITH A TORN MENISCUS

I have been running for about 35 years. These last few years, I have slowed down – Well, I'm getting older and gaining weight and getting lazier. What else can I say? Actually, my doctor told me I should quit running, because of the arthritis in my knees. That has been ten years ago already. I have not really been able to quit, but I have slowed down. I used to use DMSO and olive oil when I was competing in the 10K races and half marathon races, especially when I was really hurting. I continued to run, even though I hurt a lot. I really enjoyed running.

Several years ago, I was running and walking in one of the charity events, and two days later I ended up with a lot of pain in my left knee. I really could not walk. I had to cancel a trip to Las Vegas, Nevada, so you know I really was hurting. Anyway, I limped to Presbyterian Hospital in Albuquerque and had an x-ray taken of my knees. What had happened was I tore the meniscus in my left knee.

The meniscus is cartilage that is there to help provide cushioning and help with movement of the knee socket. When the cartilage tore, it was scraping the joint wall, and whenever it touched one of the pits or scars of the arthritis, it was oh, so painful! I was told I really needed arthroscopic surgery, because my knees were so bad with arthritis, and now with the torn cartilage I really needed the surgery. When I found out the price of the surgery (about $5,000), I thought I had better get that done at the Veterans Administration

Hospital, because I get some help since I am a Veteran of one of the old wars (Korean). I limped to the V.A. Hospital, and they told me the same thing – "You need arthroscopic surgery, especially on your left knee." I said, "OK," but they told me I would have to wait thirty to forty days until the surgical team came back from Iraq.

I was a little disappointed, but I also wasn't too anxious to get my knees cut into and cleaned out. So, I went home to wait and contemplate my dilemma. In the meantime, I thought I would try something I had used sparingly when I was running in a lot of races. No, it wasn't the DMSO, because that is almost strictly a painkiller. I have never taken any pills for the pain, but I had some extra virgin olive oil that I spread liberally on my knees. I fashioned an oil guard of some old socks and put them on my knees to help hold the oil in my knee area.

I did not notice any change in the first two days. The third day, I was able to walk with very little pain. The fourth day, I had no pain, but I walked slowly because I didn't want to awaken the torn cartilage. Well, the torn cartilage never did act up, but when I bent my knee, I could still hear something in my left knee like I was going over a bump, but it didn't hurt. I started running, and by the sixth day I was doing some pretty fast sprints. I really could not believe how good my knees felt. And today, years later, they are the best part of me. Also, with lubricating the knees, my arthritis has subsided. I used to do knee bends and I could hear the crunching of the arthritis. I cannot hear any of that now!

I have since devoloped a drink with the virgin olive oil that gets to all the joints in the body and lubricates the cartlidge and the bone in the joints. With the lubrication the olive oil provides we can move the joints easier all the time. Right now I don't have any crunching in my joints nor do I have any pain whatsoever. I never did have the orthoscopic surgery. I not only saved a lot of money but I saved my knees from the knife----It must be mentioned here that most pain management pills for arthritis do nothing to solve the problem arthritis causes.

"The Drink"

½ cup of hot water

1 tablespoon of vinegar

1 tablespoon of honey

4 tablespoons of extra virgin olive oil

3 tablespoons of flaxseed meal

This drink is to be taken once a day for three weeks. It has the vinegar and a sweetener to make the drink palatable. The flaxseed meal, which is a great omega 3 provider, helps mix the water, olive oil, vinegar, and sweetener.

This makes for a better tasting drink. You should feel results in the recommended three-week period.

I have shared my formula with many, and I have heard of so many successful outcomes.

In the final analysis, the fact that I was able to cut the pain to my knee and fully recover (after surgery had been recommended as the only thing that would allow me to walk again) is quite a breakthrough.

It's not my intention to bash on all drugs. There are some real miracle drugs that have been developed lately, but we must be aware about the side effects of many of them. I am most suspicious of pain management drugs. They really don't solve any problem, but they do a good job of masking the problem. If you mask the illness, you won't be able to identify what ails you.

My wish is that those of you who have arthritis will find as much comfort as I have using the olive oil method. I look forward to hearing your feedback!

"You can have everything you want out of life, **if you help enough other people** get what they want out of life."

– Zig Ziglar, American author, salesman and motivational speaker

Glucosamine No Better Than Placebo in Study

By Jeannine Stein
Los Angeles Times

LOS ANGELES — Many people who suffer with lower back pain rely on glucosamine supplements for some relief. But does the stuff really work? A new study shows that glucosamine was no different from a placebo in treating lower back pain.

The study, released Tuesday in the Journal of the American Medical Association, was a large, double-blind, randomized placebo-controlled trial that included 250 adults with chronic lower back pain. It was conducted at the Oslo University Outpatient Clinic in Norway.

Chronic lower back pain plagues millions of people in the United States, and treatments include physical therapy, medication and the use of glucosamine supplements. Glucosamine is naturally produced by the body and is found in healthy cartilage. Glucosamine supplements (usually combined with chondroitin) are typically taken for the pain and discomfort that accompanies osteoarthritis, because they are thought to restore cartilage and reduce inflammation.

Some studies have shown the supplement to be effective in treating some joint pain, but others show no benefit.

Among the participants in this study, half were randomly assigned to take 1,500 milligrams of glucosamine for six months, while the other half took a placebo for the same amount of time.

Studies: Arthritis Not Worth Knee Surgery

■ *Researchers say medication, therapy just as effective*

By Linda A. Johnson
The Associated Press

Two studies call into question whether many people with arthritis are needlessly undergoing one of the most common operations in America: arthroscopic knee surgery.

One finds that surgery is no better than medication and physical therapy for relieving the pain and stiffness of moderate or severe arthritis. The other reveals that tears in knee cartilage — which often prompt such surgeries — are very common without causing symptoms.

Experts said the new studies and other evidence show that arthroscopic knee surgery still has a place, such as after a recent injury, but shouldn't be done routinely for osteoarthritis.

"A lot of people would prefer physical therapy and their doctors would as well," said Dr. E. Anthony Rankin, spokesman for the American Academy of Orthopedic Surgeons.

The studies were published in today's New England Journal of Medicine.

Nearly 27 million Americans have osteoarthritis, a top cause of disability. Symptoms usually begin after age 40 and progress as a breakdown of cartilage on the end of bones causes them to rub together at joints, leading to stiffness and pain and limiting movement.

One popular solution is arthroscopic surgery, in which a scope with a miniature camera is inserted through a tiny incision and surgeons operate through other tiny cuts. Surgeons typically smooth damaged cartilage surfaces on the bone's ends and flush out bone chips.

This allows quicker healing than traditional surgery, but can still trigger blood clots, infection and nerve or blood vessel damage.

About 1 million arthroscopic knee surgeries are done in this country each year, costing roughly $7,000, depending on the location, when done as an outpatient procedure.

A large study in 2002 found the operation was no better than sham surgery, but the procedure remains popular.

Some experts think the increased use of MRIs to diagnose knee problems could be leading to unnecessary surgeries or at least referrals to orthopedic surgeons.

32

Z-CoiL
Pain Relief Footwear

Unsolicited Customer Testimonials

I have had plantar fasciitis in my left foot now for four years. I have had PT, cortisone shots, hard casts and soft (air boot) casts, and now Laser treatments, and I am still wearing my orthotics. I still have trouble at night and in the morning when not wearing any shoes. I have heard good and bad things about having the surgery and the doctors also say there is no guarantee. I also have a condition called Reflex Symptomatic Dystrophy (RSD) which is basically severe nerve pain that kicks in when I have any kind of procedure done.

I wind up in the hospital on a morphine drip for about 3-4 days, then it goes away. So you can see why I don't want to choose the surgery road.

After wearing the air boot on a daily basis—which also messes up your alignment—my friends at work told me to go and try the Z-CoiL shoes. I had already tried 32 different pairs of tennis shoes and was hesitant about trying another. Well, I thought they looked goofy, but I was willing to try anything at this point. I found the Z-CoiL Pain Relief Footwear store in Millersville, Maryland.

I have been wearing the Blue and White Freedom for 16 hours a day now and I just went back and bought the Tia work dress shoe. With Z-CoiL shoes you will have the ability to be able to walk again with no pain! What a difference they have made in my life! Yes, they still look goofy to other people—but hey, I don't care, because they work. The coils take the pressure off my heel and enable me to walk and stand.

Penny Cauffiel
Kensington, Maryland

I have had flat foot reconstructive surgery on both of my feet. They would ache terribly when I spent long amounts of time on them. I have been unable to control the pain with expensive orthotics.

I saw a waitress wearing Z-CoiL shoes while on vacation. I was immediately interested when she told me she could be on her feet for long periods without pain. A Z-CoiL dealer was just down the road. My family was going to a theme park the next day and I figured I would have to rent a power cart because of the pain. I purchased Z-Walkers and got used to them on my way back to the car. I wore them all day at the theme park the next day with no aches! What a blessing!

I just saw my podiatrist and told him about my Z-CoiL shoes. I told him he needed to sell these! I have found a local dealership and will contact them to buy a dress pair. Thanks for your dedication!

Susan Loomis
Greenville, Michigan

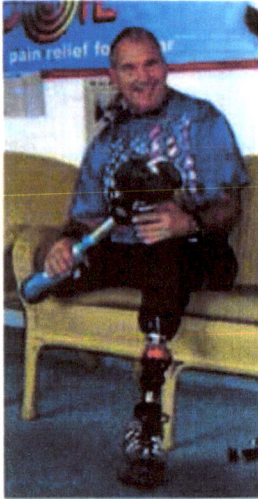

In January 2005, as a result of a double leg amputation related to my prior military service, I visited the Walter Reed Hospital in Washington, D.C. I went for new artificial legs with more shock absorption and more mobility. The rehabilitation staff was curious about my own shock absorption system: Z-CoiL footwear. I purchased them in Prescott, Arizona nearly two years ago and have worn them daily since then.

Z-CoiL footwear work for the human body like a suspension system does for an automobile. The hospital staff agreed, after days of laboratory gait testing, that my Z-CoiL footwear does significantly reduce shock of impact where the sockets of my new prosthetics attach to my own legs. This greatly reduces pain in the attachment area.

Thanks to the personal fitting process that is part of the Z-CoiL experience, my shoes fit just right and do what I need them to do. They provide cushioning and stability. I can stay on my legs for 20 hours at a time now as opposed to 8-10 hours pre-Z-CoiL shoes.

The Walter Reed staff's interest is for all veterans who deal daily with pain issues in the feet, ankles, legs, hips, and back. However, I know that pain relief is more than an issue for just veterans, as anyone will get pain relief using this unique and personally-fitted orthotic footwear. My entire family wears Z-CoiL shoes and I highly recommend that anyone seeking pain relief in the feet, legs, or back give them a try. They have made a big difference for me; just imagine what they could do for you!

Tom Lopeman
Walker, Arizona

Simply Amazing! I CAN WALK AGAIN! Before I got my Z-CoiL shoes, I had to get a wheelchair just for simple shopping visits. I'm only 18! How embarrassing. Now when I go out wearing my Z-CoiL shoes, I get

compliments about how cool my shoes are and I feel as if I can walk for an eternity! My pain medication intake has greatly decreased and I finally feel and look my age.

Since turning 14, I have had two back surgeries and six back injections and was facing a third back surgery to fix a ruptured disc. I have a genetic disc disorder and my spinal discs herniate and rupture about every two years. Now no doctor will touch me because I'm so young and have already had too much work done. I finally got a pair of Z-CoiL shoes, and it's the only thing that has helped me.

The people who sold me these shoes at the Z-CoiL store in Irving, Texas, were just wonderful. They were so very kind and understanding and just great people. I will definitely be a regular customer.

What can I say? Amazing shoes, GREAT customer service—what more can a person ask for? I will certainly be wearing Z-CoiL shoes until my time is up.

Megan Bantau
Little Elm, Texas

This is only a small sampling of the hundreds of unsolicited testimonials we have received from our customers. To read many, many more, visit our website at www.zcoil.com and select "Testimonials."

www.zcoil.com

TESTIMONIALS

August 19, 2010

Testimonial of Brendalee Kirschenman

"I purchased my first pair of Z-CoiLs in March, 2010. Before I came into the Z-Coil Store, my pain issues covered many areas, including my back, knees, shoulder and neck. I have arthritis throughout my body.

I had extreme pain in my back and knees. My doctor sent me to a surgeon to discuss what could be done about my knees. The surgeon said there was no hope, the only solution was knee replacement and in the meantime I could have cortisone shots at $300 a shot and not covered by health care.

My mother had bought a pair of Z-CoiLs and raved about them, because she has had two knee replacements and two back operations and walked with a walker. (See Gladys Kirschenman testimonial). I didn't believe that a shoe could make that much difference for her, and I said someone was taking her for a ride. Then, after months of her nagging me, I came in to try them on. The first time I tried them on, I cried, as the pain was GONE immediately. I started walking around the store and I just couldn't believe that I had no pain. I walked down the street and still no pain. Before this, I was in the house all the time in excruciating pain and not able to work because of the pain. I was too embarrassed to tell people that I was on morphine for the pain, so I just stayed in the house as much as possible.

I now own three pairs of Z-CoiLs, two pairs of runners and one pair of sandals. These are the 1st pair of sandals that I've been able to wear in over 10 years, with comfort and no pain. Since purchasing my shoes, my shoulder hasn't given me any pain, either.

I no longer have to take morphine for the pain. I promote Z-CoiL footwear as much as I can because I believe in them so much!

I thank god every day for giving Al Gallegos, who invented these shoes, the knowledge to do so, which has changed my life completely. I am no longer stuck in bed and in the house all the time. I can not go out and walk my dog; I have even walked up to six kilometers in one day with no pain medication! I wear my Z-CoiLs every waking hour and will not wear any other shoes. My husband has even bought me a cell phone, as I am no longer in the house all the time and he never knows where to find me."

Brendalee Kirschenman

Red Deer, Alberta, Canada

August 24, 2010

Testimonial of Arturo Caballero

Dear Mr. Alvaro Z. Gallegos and Andres Gallegos:

"I have been dealing with a condition called sacrolitis and neuropathy since the year 2000. I have tried all kinds of medical therapies to treat my excruciating pain over the past decade: acupuncture, massage, Steroid injections, chiropractor, powerful medications, physical therapy, and pool therapy. I had hit a dead end.

On 08/20/10, I bought a pair of anniversary shoes and I am shocked at the positive results of this medical device affords me. It's incredible.

I would like to present to my employer a full leather shoe for their approval in the work area; however, at this time I am unable to afford them since I just bought a pair of size 13 Anniversary model. Do you have any different pairs of ZCoil Shoes to see what helps my medical condition the most that way I will know what pair to buy in the future. Mr. Gallegos is god sent for inventing this dev ice since living with pain is a crazy way to live. I wear the shoes everywhere I go and people ask me allot about this shoe. I tell them the incredible pain relief the shoe give me. I have made sure they go away with the name ZCOIL."

Arturo Caballero

SO?

So much money is spent on health care in our lifetime as the article on the next page points out. So, I say – The best alternative to having to spend so much money on health care is to get healthy! We can start by eating healthy foods, by not smoking, and by exercising. A tall order, yes, but it gets to be a neat challenge.

If your body hurts when you walk briskly or run, use of footwear, like Z-CoiLs that reduce the impact on your body, as much as 50%, when you walk or run. Always stretch properly before every exercise.

Soon, you'll be loving it!

This guy didn't need Z-CoiLs

But we caught him wearing Z-CoiLs!

Foot Facts

According to the U.S. National Center for Health Statistics, impairment of the lower extremities is a leading cause of activity limitation in older people. As if foot problems weren't enough of a nuisance, they can also lead to knee, hip and lower back pain that undermine mobility just as effectively. The NCHS says one-fourth of all nursing home patients cannot walk at all and another one-sixth can walk only with assistance.

(Source: NCHS)

The human foot has been called the "mirror of health." Foot doctors, or doctors of podiatric medicine (DPMs), are often the first doctors to see signs of such systemic conditions as diabetes, arthritis, and circulatory disease in the foot.

more than
300
number of different foot ailments

Source: APMA

The Foot Facts by the US National Center for Health Statistics are very revealing. It talks about how important our feet are for our well being and our over all health. That means, we should all be wearing a shoe that is very supportive and offers great cushioning.

The Z-CoiL shoe does that!